MARONITE
LENTEN COMPANION

a

*Spiritual Journey to
the Harbour of Salvation*

Edited by Mikaël Simon-Thompson.

Table of Contents

Cana Sunday	1
Second Sunday of Lent	7
Third Sunday of Lent	13
Fourth Sunday of Lent	19
Fifth Sunday of Lent	25
Sixth Sunday of Lent	31
Hosanna Sunday	35
Monday of Holy Week	43
Tuesday of Holy Week	49
Wednesday of Holy Week	53
Thursday of Holy Week	57
Friday Signing of the Chalice	61
Friday Burial of Our Lord	65
Saturday of the Light	71
Resurrection Sunday	79
Daily Morning & Evening Prayer	85

The Sundays of Lent

Scripture Readings, Prayers, & Meditations from the Fathers

Entrance into the Great Lent
The Wedding at Cana

SEDRO

O Christ, the Only Begotten Son,
on this day you chose to sit among the invited guests,
enriching them with the abundance of your divine gifts.

As your disciples believed that you are the Messiah,
the Son of the Living God,
we also believe in you.

In place of the old Law, you have given us your new Gospel,
and instead of the fruit of the vine,
you have quenched our thirst
with the chalice of your redeeming blood.

Now, O Lord, we ask you,
with the fragrance of this incense,
and through the intercession of your Virgin Mother,
whose request you grant,
that we may always drink of your holy wine,
quenching our thirst with your heavenly love.

May your light shine in the world,
and may we know that you are the spring of living water
from which we may drink.

O Lord, bless our families and our Lenten journey,
that we may reach the harbour of salvation,
which is the glorious feast of your Resurrection.

We glorify and thank you,
your Father, and your Holy Spirit,
forever.

MZMOORO

You brought joy to the guests, Lord, when you made the water wine. Make us glad at your banquet, when your majesty will shine. Let your servants, Lord, thank you, for you made the water wine. Let your saints glorify you, when your majesty will shine. Lord our God, you accepted what the just had offered you. Now accept in your mercy our pure sacrifice and prayers.

READING

Romans 14:14–23

Brothers and Sisters:
I know and am persuaded in the Lord Jesus that nothing is unclean in itself; but it is unclean for anyone who thinks it unclean.

If your brother or sister is being injured by what you eat, you are no longer walking in love. Do not let what you eat cause the ruin of one for whom Christ died. So do not let your good be spoken of as evil.

For the kingdom of God is not food and drink but righteousness and peace and joy in the Holy Spirit. The one who thus serves Christ is acceptable to God and has human approval.

Let us then pursue what makes for peace and for mutual upbuilding. Do not, for the sake of food, destroy the work of God. Everything is indeed clean, but it is wrong for you to make others fall by what you eat; it is good not to eat meat or drink wine or do anything that makes your brother or sister stumble.

The faith that you have, have as your own conviction before God. Blessed are those who have no reason to condemn themselves because of what they approve.

But those who have doubts are condemned if they eat, because they do not act from faith; for whatever does not proceed from faith is sin.

Praise be to God always!

HOLY GOSPEL

John 2:1–11 The Wedding at Cana

Let us be attentive to the Gospel of Life and Salvation of our Lord Jesus Christ as recorded by the apostle John.

The Apostle John writes:

On the third day there was a wedding in Cana of Galilee, and the mother of Jesus was there. Jesus and his disciples had also been invited to the wedding.

When the wine gave out, the mother of Jesus said to him, "They have no wine." And Jesus said to her, "Woman, what concern is that to you and to me? My hour has not yet come." His mother said to the servants, "Do whatever he tells you."

Now standing there were six stone water jars for the Jewish rites of purification, each holding twenty or thirty gallons. Jesus said to them, "Fill the jars with water." And they filled them up to the brim.

He said to them, "Now draw some out, and take it to the chief steward." So they took it.

When the steward tasted the water that had become wine, and did not know where it came from (though the servants who had drawn the water knew), the steward called the bridegroom and said to him, "Everyone serves the good wine first, and then the inferior wine after the guests have become drunk. But you have kept the good wine until now."

Jesus did this, the first of his signs, in Cana of Galilee, and revealed his glory; and his disciples believed in him.

This is the truth.

✠ Peace be with you.

MEDITATION FROM THE SYRIAC FATHERS

I have invited you, Lord, to a feast of hymns!
The wine—a discourse of praise—has run out in our feast! The one whose vessels are full of good wine is invited! May your song fill my mouth!

Refrain: Glory to you from all who perceive your truth!

Wine in vessels is similar—of the same kind.
But this is speech-endowed wine, which begets praise.
This wine has begotten praise
Among drinkers who have seen a marvel!

It was indeed right that at someone else's feast,
You filled six vessels with good wine.
In this feast, instead of vessels,
Lord, fill a myriad of ears with delight!

Jesus was invited to the feast of others.
Look: your pure and fair feast has gladdened your guests! For behold, those you invited, Lord, need
Your songs: let your lyre speak!

Your bride is your soul, and your body is your bridal chamber. Your invited guests are the senses, with the

thoughts. And if one body has become your banquet,
Your feast is the Church, being complete.

The Holy One wedded the synagogue on Mount Sinai.
Its body gleamed in white garments, but its heart was dark. It slept with the calf, and the Exalted One despised it, And broke the tablets—the book of its covenant.

Who has ever seen such a calamity in the midst of a shameful deed? The bride, as she defiled her bridal chamber, raised her voice. She had dwelt in Egypt, where she learned of Joseph's pursuer, Who cried out though she had sinned.

The light of the pillar—fire and cloud—Drew its rays within itself, Like the sun that was darkened On the day the bride called out to the king, claiming another crime.

How, Lord, shall my lyre keep your song quiet?
And how has my tongue taught about iniquity?
Your love has given confidence to the shamed,
Yet my will is iniquitous!

It is right for humans to give thanks to your divinity.
It is right for those exalted to worship your humanity.
The exalted marvel at how small you have become.
The earthly marvel at how exalted you have become.

> Ephrem the Syrian, Hymns on Faith, Hymn 14

Second Sunday of Lent
Cleansing of the Leper

SEDRO

O Christ our God, Physician of souls and bodies, in your plan of salvation you had pity on the leper who was outcast, and healed him by your word.

We lift up our eyes and hearts to you at all times, and we implore you never to keep your mercy and grace from us, but to look upon us with compassion as you did with the leper. Cleanse us and make us holy.

Now, O Lord, we ask you, with the fragrance of this incense, to stretch forth your hand and have compassion on us. For you have said, Ask, and it will be given to you. Seek, and you will find. Knock, and the door will be opened for you.

With unfailing hope, we implore you to forgive our sins in your love, and heal us in your grace. Accept those who repent, and bring back those who have gone astray. Console the grieving, and strengthen the weak. Satisfy the hungry, and provide for those in need. Bless those who are generous, and enrich them with good deeds.

Remember the departed who have gone to their rest hoping in you. We raise glory and thanks to you, to your Father, and to your Holy Spirit forever.

MZMOORO

The poor leper begged Jesus, If you choose, Lord, make me clean, and his prayer touched our Lord's heart. He then told him, Be made clean. Christ our Lord, our

Physician, you have made the leper clean. Now we beg you to heal us, by your word forgive our sins. Lord our God, you accepted what the just had offered you. Now accept, in your mercy, our pure sacrifice and prayers.

READING

Romans 6:12–23

Brothers and Sisters:
Do not let sin exercise dominion in your mortal bodies, to make you obey their passions.

No longer present your members to sin as instruments of wickedness, but present yourselves to God as those who have been brought from death to life, and present your members to God as instruments of righteousness.

For sin will have no dominion over you, since you are not under law but under grace. What then? Should we sin because we are not under law but under grace? By no means!

Do you not know that if you present yourselves to anyone as obedient slaves, you are slaves of the one whom you obey, either of sin, which leads to death, or of obedience, which leads to righteousness?

But thanks be to God that you, having once been slaves of sin, have become obedient from the heart to the form of teaching to which you were entrusted, and that you, having been set free from sin, have become slaves of righteousness.

I am speaking in human terms because of your natural limitations. For just as you once presented your members as slaves to impurity and to greater and greater iniquity, so now present your members as slaves to righteousness for sanctification.

When you were slaves of sin, you were free in regard to righteousness. So what advantage did you then get from the things of which you now are ashamed? The end of those things is death.

But now that you have been freed from sin and enslaved to God, the advantage you get is sanctification. The end is eternal life.

For the wages of sin is death, but the free gift of God is eternal life in Christ Jesus our Lord.

Praise be to God always!

HOLY GOSPEL

Mark 1:35–43 The Cleansing of a Leper

Let us be attentive to the Gospel of Life and Salvation of our Lord Jesus Christ as recorded by the evangelist Mark.

The Evangelist Mark writes:

In the morning, while it was still very dark, he got up and went out to a deserted place, and there he prayed.

And Simon and his companions hunted for him. When they found him, they said to him, "Everyone is searching for you."

He answered, "Let us go on to the neighbouring towns, so that I may proclaim the message there also; for that is what I came out to do."

And he went throughout Galilee, proclaiming the message in their synagogues and casting out demons.

A leper came to him begging him, and kneeling he said to him, "If you choose, you can make me clean."

Moved with pity, Jesus stretched out his hand and touched him, and said to him, "I do choose. Be made clean!"

Immediately the leprosy left him, and he was made clean. After sternly warning him he sent him away at once.

This is the truth.

✠ Peace be with you.

MEDITATION FROM THE SYRIAC FATHERS

And what indeed can be so surprising if those who came to the Lord and were intimately associated with Him received His power, as we see when the Apostles preached the Word of God and the Spirit fell upon those believers? Cornelius received power from the Word of God when he heard it. How much more, in the case of the Lord speaking with Mary or Zacchaeus, or to the sinful woman who let her hair down and wiped the feet of the Lord, or with the Samaritan woman or the good thief—did not power go out and the Holy Spirit mingle with the souls?

Now those who pursue God in love, having abandoned everything else, and who persevere in prayer, are taught secretly things they had not known before. For truth itself comes to them according to their desire, and it teaches them.

"I am the truth" (Jn 14:6). Even the Apostles themselves, before the crucifixion, staying close to the Lord, saw great miracles—namely, how lepers were cleansed and the dead raised to life. But they did not yet know how the divine power operates or ministers in the heart. They did not yet know that they had to be reborn spiritually, be joined with the heavenly soul, and become a new creature. Because of the signs that He performed, they loved the Lord. But the Lord told them: "Why do you marvel at such signs? I give you a great inheritance which the whole world does not possess."

However, these words were strange to them until He arose from the dead and ascended with His body into heaven for us. And then the Spirit, the Comforter, entered and mingled with them. The Truth in person shows Himself to the faithful. And the heavenly Man walks with you and forms one fellowship.

Whoever, therefore, dedicates themselves to different forms of service and eagerly performs all such activities, motivated by zeal, faith, and love of God, that very service, after a while, leads them to a knowledge of truth itself. For the Lord appears to their souls and teaches them how the Holy Spirit operates.

Glory and adoration to the Father and the Son and the Holy Spirit forever. Amen.

The Macarian Homilies, Homily 12

Third Sunday of Lent
Healing the Haemorrhaging Woman

SEDRO

All-powerful and Almighty Father, long ago you spoke to your ancestors in various ways, but at the appointed time you sent your beloved Son to us. Through His words and miracles, He taught us about you and commanded us to love one another.

We thank you for all that you have given us through your Son, our Lord Jesus Christ. We glorify you, O Father, the Lord of life and salvation. You are the Holy One who knows what lies in the hearts of those who love you, and you heal the pains of those who take refuge in you. As your Only Begotten Son healed the paralytic and the blind man, the hemorrhaging woman and the lame man, heal us and fill our souls with calm and peace as your Son calmed the surging waves.

Now, O Lord, we implore you with the fragrance of this incense for all those who are suffering. Pour the balm of your consolation on their wounded hearts. Watch over them with your fatherly eyes. Rest in their trials and suffering they stray from your love. Raise your right hand and bless also those who are healthy, so that joy may dwell in the hearts of all. We raise glory and praise to you, to your Son, and to your Holy Spirit forever.

MZMOORO

In great anguish a woman came to Christ and touched his cloak. While the crowds pressed round him, she was cured and made it known. Here, O peoples and nations, she approached and touched his cloak. All on earth be attentive, she was cured and made it known. Lord our God, you accepted what the just had offered you. Now accept in your mercy our pure sacrifice and prayers.

READING

2 Corinthians 7:4–11

Brothers and Sisters:
I often boast about you; I have great pride in you; I am filled with consolation; I am overjoyed in all our affliction.

For even when we came into Macedonia, our bodies had no rest, but we were afflicted in every way — disputes without and fears within.

But God, who consoles the downcast, consoled us by the arrival of Titus, and not only by his coming, but also by the consolation with which he was consoled about you, as he told us of your longing, your mourning, your zeal for me, so that I rejoiced still more.

For even if I made you sorry with my letter, I do not regret it (though I did regret it, for I see that I grieved you with that letter, though only briefly).

Now I rejoice, not because you were grieved, but because your grief led to repentance; for you felt a godly grief, so that you were not harmed in any way by us.

For godly grief produces a repentance that leads to salvation and brings no regret, but worldly grief produces death.

For see what earnestness this godly grief has produced in you, what eagerness to clear yourselves, what indignation, what alarm, what longing, what zeal, what punishment! At every point you have proved yourselves guiltless in the matter.

Praise be to God always!

HOLY GOSPEL

Luke 8:40–56 The Healing of the Haemorrhaging Woman

Let us be attentive to the Gospel of Life and Salvation of our Lord Jesus Christ as recorded by the evangelist Luke.

The Evangelist Luke writes:

When Jesus returned, the crowd welcomed him, for they were all waiting for him.

Just then there came a man named Jairus, a leader of the synagogue. He fell at Jesus' feet and begged him to come to his house, for he had an only daughter, about twelve years old, who was dying.

As he went, the crowds pressed in on him. Now there was a woman who had been suffering from hemorrhages for twelve years; and though she had spent all she had on physicians, no one could cure her.

She came up behind him and touched the fringe of his clothes, and immediately her hemorrhage stopped.

Then Jesus asked, "Who touched me?" When all denied it, Peter said, "Master, the crowds surround you and press in on you."

But Jesus said, "Someone touched me; for I noticed that power had gone out from me."

When the woman saw that she could not remain hidden, she came trembling; and falling down before him, she declared in the presence of all the people why she had touched him, and how she had been immediately healed.

He said to her, "Daughter, your faith has made you well; go in peace."

While he was still speaking, someone came from the leader's house to say, "Your daughter is dead; do not trouble the teacher any longer."

When Jesus heard this, he replied, "Do not fear. Only believe, and she will be saved."

When he came to the house, he did not allow anyone to enter with him, except Peter, John, and James, and the child's father and mother. They were all weeping and wailing for her; but he said, "Do not weep; for she is not dead but sleeping."

And they laughed at him, knowing that she was dead. But he took her by the hand and called out, "Child, get up!"

Her spirit returned, and she got up at once. Then he directed them to give her something to eat. Her parents were astounded; but he ordered them to tell no one what had happened.

This is the truth.

✠ Peace be with you.

MEDITATION FROM THE SYRIAC FATHERS

If anyone stands solely on his own righteousness and redemption, he labors in vain and to no purpose. For every fancy of one's own justification will appear on the last day as a filthy rag, as the Prophet Isaiah says: "All our justification has been as a filthy rag" (Is 64:6). Let us, then, beg and implore God to clothe us with "the garment of salvation" (Is 61:10), namely, our Lord Jesus Christ, the ineffable Light, which those who have borne it will never put off for all eternity. But in the resurrection their bodies also will be glorified by the glory of the Light with which the faithful and noble persons are even now clothed, as the Apostle says: "He that raised up Christ from the dead will also raise up our mortal bodies by his Spirit that dwells in us" (Rom 8:11). Glory to His ineffable compassion and His ineffable mercy.

And again, just as the woman afflicted with an issue of blood believed truly and touched the hem of the garment of the Lord and immediately received a healing and the flow of the unclean fountain of blood dried up, so everyone afflicted by the incurable wound of sin—the fountain of unclean and evil thoughts—if he only approaches Christ and begs prayerfully and truly believes in Him, receives a salvific healing from the incurable fountain of passions. That fountain, which has been sending up unclean thoughts, now fails and dries up through the power of Jesus alone. For nothing else can cure this wound.

For no earthly medicines—that is, mankind's own justifying actions—had any power to cure the human race of so great an interior plague. But this could be done only by the heavenly and divine nature of the so great gift of the Holy Spirit. Man could be healed only by the help of this medicine and thus could attain life by a cleansing of his heart by the Holy Spirit.

However, just as that woman, although afflicted, could not yet be cured, she still had feet by which she could hasten to the Lord, and, approaching Him, she obtained a cure. Likewise, as that blind man, even though he could not approach and come to the Lord because he had no sight, yet he let out a cry, swifter than the angels, saying, "Son of David, have mercy on me" (Mk 10:47), and so believing he received his healing by the Lord's coming to him and restoring his sight. So too, a person, even though he is heavily afflicted by evil passions and is blinded by the darkness of sin, nevertheless still possesses the ability to will to cry out and beg Jesus that He come and bring eternal salvation to his soul.

The Macarian Homilies, Homily 20

Fourth Sunday of Lent
The Parable of the Prodigal Son

SEDRO

O Christ our God, You are the true light who has come into the world. You are the way that leads to the Father, and no one comes to the Father except through You. You showed us Your love when You lived among us, and You told us of the Father's compassion and His love for repentant sinners. You spoke to us of repentance, of mercy, and of living water. Today we meditate on the parable of the prodigal son who, trusting his father, turned from his life of corruption and repented of his sin.

Now, O Lord, we ask You, with the fragrance of this incense, to have compassion on us, as You have compassion on all sinners. May we humble ourselves before You and repent of our sins. Enlighten us that we may know You. Strengthen us with Your power, and do not turn Your face away from us, lest the darkness of sin surround us. Send Your Spirit to us sinners during this forgiving season of Lent, so that we may return to You by seeking forgiveness.

Open Your blessed arms to us and bring us close to You, so that we may meet You with joy and find happiness in knowing You. Be our strength and our help, that we may glorify You, Your Father, and Your Holy Spirit forever.

MZMOORO

The true love of the father far surpassed his son's great sin. He ran out to embrace him when at last his son came home. I have sinned against heaven and before you, said the son, though my heart now condemns me. You are greater than my heart. Lord our God, you accepted what the just had offered you. Now accepting your mercy are pure sacrifice and prayers.

READING

2 Corinthians 13:5–13

Brothers and Sisters:
Examine yourselves to see whether you are living in the faith. Test yourselves. Do you not realize that Jesus Christ is in you? — unless, indeed, you fail to meet the test! I hope you will find out that we have not failed.

But we pray to God that you may not do anything wrong — not that we may appear to have met the test, but that you may do what is right, though we may seem to have failed.

For we cannot do anything against the truth, but only for the truth. For we rejoice when we are weak and you are strong. This is what we pray for, that you may become perfect.

So I write these things while I am away from you, so that when I come, I may not have to be severe in using the authority that the Lord has given me for building up and not for tearing down.

Finally, brothers and sisters, farewell. Put things in order, listen to my appeal, agree with one another, live in peace; and the God of love and peace will be with you. Greet one another with a holy kiss. All the saints greet you. The grace of the Lord Jesus Christ, the love of God, and the communion of the Holy Spirit be with all of you.

Praise be to God always!

HOLY GOSPEL

Luke 15:11–32 The Parable of the Lost Son

Let us be attentive to the Gospel of Life and Salvation of our Lord Jesus Christ as recorded by the evangelist Luke.

The Lord Jesus says:
"There was a man who had two sons. The younger said to his father, 'Father, give me my share of the property.' So he divided it between them.

A few days later the younger son took all he had and went to a distant country, squandering it in dissolute living. When he had spent everything, a severe famine arose, and he became in need. He hired himself to a citizen there to feed pigs, longing to eat what the pigs ate, but no one gave him anything.

When he came to himself, he said, 'How many of my father's hired hands have bread enough, and here I am dying of hunger! I will go to my father and say, "Father, I have sinned against heaven and you; I am no longer worthy to be called your son. Treat me like a hired hand."' So he set off to his father.

While he was still far off, his father saw him, ran, embraced, and kissed him. The son said, 'Father, I have sinned against heaven and you; I am no longer worthy to be called your son.' But the father said to his servants, 'Bring the best robe, put a ring on his finger and sandals on his feet. Kill the fatted calf and celebrate, for this son was dead and is alive again; he was lost and is found!'

Now the elder son was in the field. When he heard music and dancing, he asked a servant what was happening. The servant said, 'Your brother has returned; your father has killed the fatted calf to celebrate.' The elder son became angry and refused to enter. His father pleaded with him, but he answered, 'For all these years I have served you and never disobeyed, yet you never gave me even a young goat to celebrate with my friends. But this son of yours, who squandered your property with prostitutes, you killed the fatted calf for him!'

The father said, 'Son, you are always with me, and all that is mine is yours. But we had to celebrate and rejoice, for this brother of yours was dead and is alive again; he was lost and is found."'

This is the truth.

✠ Peace be with you.

MEDITATION FROM THE SYRIAC FATHERS

The Lord's mercy is everlasting, and His justice reaches to the ends of the earth. He rescues the captive, restores the lost, and heals the brokenhearted. Those who trust in Him shall not be shaken, and their faith shall be their shield. The glory of the Lord is beyond measure, and His works are full of wonder and majesty. All creation gives Him praise: the birds of the air, the beasts of the field, the fish of the seas, and all that move upon the earth. The voice of the Lord is in the wind and in the thunder, and His presence fills the world with awe. Blessed is the man who fears the Lord, who delights in His commandments and walks in His ways, for he shall be established in righteousness, and his descendants shall be blessed forever. The Lord is faithful to His covenant, and His word is true from generation to generation. The hearts of the righteous are lifted in song, and their mouths declare His glory continually. Let all who have breath praise the Lord, for His mercy endures for all time, and His truth is unchanging. He has appointed the stars and the elements, the rivers and the seas, and the winds and the seasons, and all obey His command. The mountains and valleys, the dry lands and the fertile fields, all bear witness to His order. His eyes watch over the earth, and His hand sustains every living creature. He opens His hand to the poor and fills the hungry with good things. He guards the innocent, punishes the wicked, and delivers the oppressed. The heavens declare His glory, and the firmament proclaims His handiwork. The sun rises and sets according to His word, and the night and day perform their appointed courses. His works are full of wisdom and marvel, and all creation testifies to His greatness. He gives strength to the weary, joy to the mournful, and peace to the troubled. Those who honour Him in their hearts and with their deeds are blessed, and their legacy endures. The birds of the air, the beasts of the field, and the fish of the sea praise Him. All creation sings of His mercy and justice. His covenant is eternal, His word unwavering, and His love unending. Let every soul praise the Lord, for He is holy, mighty, and true, and His faithfulness lasts forever.

> Jacob of Serug, Homily on the Prodigal Son

Fifth Sunday of Lent
Healing of the Paralytic

SEDRO

O Christ, the only begotten Son and Word of the Father, you came down to us in your mercy and compassion. You chose to show the extent of your affection and love by telling the paralytic to take up his mat and to walk in the sight of the crowd that all might believe in your divinity. You restored joy to the suffering paralytic and forgave his sins.

We thank you and praise you for the great gift that you have given to your church. In your name she absolves sins and forgives those who repent.

Now, O Christ our God, we ask you, with the fragrance of this incense, to extend your mighty hand upon us. Come to us with the power of your forgiveness. Confirm our faith in you and implant in us the memory of your divine miracles and teachings. We glorify and thank you, your Father, and your Holy Spirit, forever.

MZMOORO

The sweet voice of Christ Jesus made the paralyzed man walk. All your sins are forgiven. Take your mat and go in peace. In the church dwells the Spirit, flowing from the heart of Christ. Now we ask you, O Savior, pardon us and grant us peace. Lord our God, you accepted what the just had offered you. Now accept, to your mercy, our pure sacrifice and prayers.

READING

1 Timothy 5:24-6:5

Brothers and Sisters:
The sins of some people are conspicuous and precede them to judgment, while the sins of others follow them there. So also good works are conspicuous; and even when they are not, they cannot remain hidden.

Let all who are under the yoke of slavery regard their masters as worthy of all honor, so that the name of God and the teaching may not be blasphemed. Those who have believing masters must not be disrespectful to them on the ground that they are members of the church; rather they must serve them all the more, since those who benefit by their service are believers and beloved.

Teach and urge these duties. Whoever teaches otherwise and does not agree with the sound words of our Lord Jesus Christ and the teaching that is in accordance with godliness, is conceited, understanding nothing, and has a morbid craving for controversy and for disputes about words. From these come envy, dissension, slander, base suspicions, and wrangling among those who are depraved in mind and bereft of the truth, imagining that godliness is a means of gain.

Praise be to God always!

HOLY GOSPEL

Mark 2:1-12 Healing the Paralytic

Let us be attentive to the Gospel of Life and Salvation of our Lord Jesus Christ as recorded by the evangelist Mark.

The Evangelist Mark writes:

When Jesus returned to Capernaum after some days, it was reported that he was at home. So many gathered around that there was no longer room for them, not even in front of the door; and he was speaking the word to them. Then some people came, bringing to him a paralyzed man, carried by four of them. And when they could not bring him to Jesus because of the crowd, they removed the roof above him; and after having dug through it, they let down the mat on which the paralytic lay.

When Jesus saw their faith, he said to the paralytic, "Son, your sins are forgiven." Now some of the scribes were sitting there, questioning in their hearts, "Why does this fellow speak in this way? It is blasphemy! Who can forgive sins but God alone?"

At once Jesus perceived in his spirit that they were discussing these questions among themselves; and he said to them, "Why do you raise such questions in your hearts? Which is easier, to say to the paralytic, 'Your sins are forgiven,' or to say, 'Stand up and take your mat and walk'? But so that you may know that the Son of Man has authority on earth to forgive sins"—he said to the paralytic—"I say to you, stand up, take your mat and go to your home." And he stood up, and immediately took the mat and went out before all of them; so that they were all amazed and glorified God, saying, "We have never seen anything like this!"

This is the truth.

✠ Peace be with you.

MEDITATION FROM THE SYRIAC FATHERS

The sun, being a material, created thing, shines down also upon swampy places full of mud and slime and yet is not affected or defiled. How much more the pure and Holy Spirit that is joined to the soul which still is afflicted by evil, without himself being tainted by the evil. For: "The light shines in darkness and the darkness comprehended it not" (Jn 1:5).

When, therefore, a man is deep and rich in grace, there still remains inside of him a remnant of evil. But he has close at hand one who can help him. Wherefore, if one is overwhelmed by temptations, caught in the raging waves of passions, he ought not to lose hope. For if he acts in this way, sin builds up and takes over from within. If, however, one constantly puts his hope in God, evil to a certain degree diminishes and dries up. Certain people are afflicted with paralysis: some with mutilated members, others with fever, while others have sickness. All of this comes from sin. For sin is the root of all evils. The passions caused by the desiring powers of the soul and by evil thoughts also flow from sin. If there is a flowing spring, the places that lie in the vicinity become wet and swampy. But when hot weather comes, both the spring and the nearby areas dry up.

So also it happens to God's servants who abound in grace. For grace not only dries up the wicked desires suggested by the evil one, but also those flowing out of nature. This is because now the men of God are greater than the first Adam.

Macarian Homilies, Homily 16

Sixth Sunday of Lent
Healing of the Blind Man

SEDRO

Only begotten Word of God, born in time of the Virgin Mary, you are the Alpha and the Omega, the Beginning and the End. You chose to open the eyes of the blind to teach us that you are the Source and Giver of Light.

By your miracles, you proved that you are the awaited Messiah of whom Isaiah spoke. Then the eyes of the blind shall be opened, the lame shall leap like a deer, and the tongue of the speechless sing for joy. O Lord, who hath given us light, accept our witness and our professional faith that you are truly the Son of God and the Saviour of the world.

Now we implore you, with the fragrance of this incense, to let the light of your knowledge shine in our hearts. May we see your face and rejoice, as did Bartimaeus on the road to Jericho. And may your light shine throughout the world, so that all may see your face and rejoice in you. We raise glory to you, to your Father, who sent you, and to the Spirit, the Source of holiness, forever.

MZMOORO

Lord, my God, show your mercy, cried the blind man to our Lord. You allowed me to hear you. Let me now behold your face. Hear, O peoples and nations, what the blind man said to Christ. All on earth be attentive.

Let me now behold your face. Lord, our God, you accepted what the just had offered you. Now accept in your mercy our pure sacrifice and prayers.

READING

2 Corinthians 10:1-7

Brothers and Sisters:
I myself, Paul, appeal to you by the meekness and gentleness of Christ — I who am humble when face to face with you, but bold toward you when I am away! — I ask that when I am present I need not show boldness by daring to oppose those who think we are acting according to human standards.

Indeed, we live as human beings, but we do not wage war according to human standards; for the weapons of our warfare are not merely human, but they have divine power to destroy strongholds. We destroy arguments and every proud obstacle raised up against the knowledge of God, and we take every thought captive to obey Christ. We are ready to punish every disobedience when your obedience is complete.

Look at what is before your eyes. If you are confident that you belong to Christ, remind yourself of this, that just as you belong to Christ, so also do we.

Praise be to God always!

HOLY GOSPEL

Mark 10:46-52 The Blind Bartimaeus

Let us be attentive to the Gospel of Life and Salvation of our Lord Jesus Christ as recorded by the evangelist Mark.

The Evangelist Mark writes:

They came to Jericho. As Jesus and his disciples and a large crowd were leaving Jericho, Bartimaeus son of Timaeus, a blind beggar, was sitting by the roadside. When he heard that it was Jesus of Nazareth, he began to shout out and say, "Jesus, Son of David, have mercy on me!" Many sternly ordered him to be quiet, but he cried out even more loudly, "Son of David, have mercy on me!" Jesus stood still and said, "Call him here."

And they called the blind man, saying to him, "Take heart; get up, he is calling you." So throwing off his cloak, he sprang up and came to Jesus. Then Jesus said to him, "What do you want me to do for you?" The blind man said to him, "My teacher, let me see again." Jesus said to him, "Go; your faith has made you well." Immediately he regained his sight and followed him on the way.

This is the truth.

☩ Peace be with you.

MEDITATION FROM THE SYRIAC FATHERS

Do not be crushed by your sins. I am not saying that you should feel no pain for them; rather, you must not think they are beyond healing. It is better to be wounded than dead. Someone who is wounded can still be treated: there is a physician. On the cross, Christ pleaded for mercy for those who crucified Him. While hanging there, He asked forgiveness for His murderers.

"All manner of sin and blasphemy shall be forgiven," that is, when there is repentance. When Simon Peter denied Him and then wept, Christ forgave him. After the resurrection, He even appointed him the shepherd of His flock. Three times He asked him, "Do you love me?"—matching the three denials—in order to confirm that Peter was fully pardoned.

Christ came for sinners: to heal the brokenhearted and to bind their wounds. "The Spirit of the Lord is upon me; therefore He has anointed me to bring good news to the meek. He has sent me to bind up the brokenhearted, to proclaim freedom to captives, sight to the blind, and healing to those who are broken—through forgiveness."

The Apostle says in his letter: "Jesus Christ came into the world to save sinners." And the Lord Himself declares: "I have not come to call the righteous. Those who are well do not need a physician, but those who are sick." There were two debtors who owed a creditor; when neither could repay, he forgave them both—because they asked.

— Isaac of Nineveh, *Ascetic Homily* 65

Hosanna Sunday
Beginning of Holy Week

SEDRO

O Christ our God, in the heavens you are carried on a chariot of light, yet on earth you ride on a donkey's coat. You are hidden from the spiritual powers, yet you are praised by your holy disciples in the streets of Jerusalem.

O Holy One, you are seated on the throne of your glory, yet you are honoured by the crowds. The old and the young, infants and children, who spread their cloaks and branches before you. In your grace you have planned all this for our salvation.

Now, O Lord, we implore you, with the fragrance of this incense, to make us worthy to celebrate this feast with joy and gladness, and with reverence for your profound humility. Prepare us to go out to meet you at your second coming, with purity, wearing robes of glory, shouting with those who celebrate: "Hosanna! Blessed is he who comes in the name of the Lord." In that eternal feast, may we and our departed raise glory to you, to your Father, and to your Holy Spirit, forever.

MZMOORO

Raise your voices, be joyful, O Jerusalem, give praise, for your King humbly enters, listen and accept the truth. Zion, sing hymns of glory, O Jerusalem, give praise, for your gates have been strengthened, listen and accept the truth. Lord our God, you accepted what the just had offered you, now accept in your mercy our pure sacrifice and prayers.

READING

Philippians 1:1–13

Paul and Timothy, servants of Christ Jesus, to all the saints in Christ Jesus who are in Philippi, with the bishops and deacons: Grace to you and peace from God our Father and the Lord Jesus Christ.

I thank my God every time I remember you, constantly praying with joy in every one of my prayers for all of you, because of your sharing in the gospel from the first day until now. I am confident of this, that the one who began a good work among you will bring it to completion by the day of Jesus Christ.

It is right for me to think this way about all of you, because you hold me in your heart, for all of you share in God's grace with me, both in my imprisonment and in the defence and confirmation of the gospel. For God is my witness, how I long for all of you with the compassion of Christ Jesus.

And this is my prayer, that your love may overflow more and more with knowledge and full insight to help you to determine what is best, so that in the day of Christ you may be pure and blameless, having produced the harvest of righteousness that comes through Jesus Christ for the glory and praise of God.

I want you to know, beloved, that what has happened to me has actually helped to spread the gospel, so that it has become known throughout the whole imperial guard and to everyone else that my imprisonment is for Christ.

Praise be to God always!

HOLY GOSPEL

John 12:12–22 The Entry into Jerusalem

Let us be attentive to the Gospel of Life and Salvation of our Lord Jesus Christ as recorded by the apostle John.

The Apostle John writes:

The next day the great crowd that had come to the festival heard that Jesus was coming to Jerusalem. So they took branches of palm trees and went out to meet him, shouting, "Hosanna! Blessed is the one who comes in the name of the Lord — the King of Israel!"

Jesus found a young donkey and sat on it; as it is written: "Do not be afraid, daughter of Zion. Look, your king is coming, sitting on a donkey's colt!" His disciples did not understand these things at first; but when Jesus was glorified, then they remembered that these things had been written of him and had been done to him.

So the crowd that had been with him when he called Lazarus out of the tomb and raised him from the dead continued to testify. It was also because they heard that he had performed this sign that the crowd went to meet him. The Pharisees then said to one another, "You see, you can do nothing. Look, the world has gone after him!"

Now among those who went up to worship at the festival were some Greeks. They came to Philip, who was from Bethsaida in Galilee, and said to him, "Sir, we wish to see Jesus." Philip went and told Andrew; then Andrew and Philip went and told Jesus.

This is the truth.

✠ Peace be with you.

MEDITATION FROM THE SYRIAC FATHERS

The next day the great crowd that had come to the festival heard that Jesus was coming to Jerusalem. So they took branches of palm trees and went out to meet him, shouting: "Hosanna! Blessed is He who comes in the name of the Lord, the King of Israel!" How was it then, that though He didn't walk boldly through Judea and withdrew into the desert, He now came boldly to Jerusalem? Because their anger had abated with His withdrawal and now that it had passed He came. Besides, the crowds which preceded and followed Him were of sufficient size to worry the leaders. For no miracle disturbed them so much as that of Lazarus. Another Evangelist writes that they spread their garments at His feet and that the whole city shook from the honor accorded to His entry.

"Jesus found a young donkey and sat on it; as it is written: 'Do not be afraid, daughters of Zion. Behold, your king is coming to you, sitting on a donkey's colt!'" He did this in order to fulfill one prophecy and to prefigure another. The same event completed one and began another. "Do not be afraid, daughters of Zion. Behold, your king is coming to you, meek and sitting on a donkey's colt" was certainly the prophecy being fulfilled. By sitting on the colt of a donkey He indicated that the unclean race of the Gentiles would submit to Him.

Again, the branches of palm and olive trees and the clothes they placed on the ground demonstrate that they thought of Him more highly than a prophet and they cried to Him: "Hosanna! Blessed is he who comes in the name of the Lord." You can see that this choked the high priests and scribes more than anything, because people believed that He wasn't against God. It was this above all else that divided people: that He said He came from the Father. The prophet said "Do not be afraid, daughters of Zion, but rejoice greatly" because most of their kings had been unjust and grasping and had delivered them to their enemies. They had perverted the people and made them subservient to their foes. Thus the prophet says, "take courage – this one is not like those others. He is meek and merciful."

St. John Chrysostom

The Days of Holy Week

Scripture Readings & Prayers

Monday of Holy Week
Coming to the Harbour

PRAYER OF INCENSE

In the radiance of that Day, in the day of the Lord's Passion, fasting and prayer lead their ships to the Harbor.

O children of the all-merciful One, wake up and come forward: let us cleanse our hearts, get rid of our sins, and go to meet our Lord. Let us live by His saving Passion.

O Sea of Mercy and Compassion, in Your abundant generosity and eternal kindness, You comfort those who grieve, suffer, and seek refuge in You.

O Harbor of safety and salvation, through this incense we now offer You, be a Support and a Savior to all those who came, in true faith, to the harbor of Your holy Church. As we commemorate Your saving Passion for us, we offer glory to You, forever.

SEDRO

O God, You are the Eternal Light Who enlightened all creatures with the rays of Your revelation. You created us in Your image; You filled us with the gift of Your Holy Spirit; when we had disobeyed Your command, we were chased from the abode of life and exiled from Your Paradise. In Your eternal mercies, You had compassion on us and sent Your only Son for our salvation. In His saving and life-giving plan, He showed us the way of life to follow. He became for us a safe Guide to the true Light, He handed us a new command, the command of love, the yoke of humility and peace of conscience. In it we found absolute peace for our soul.

O Lord, with joyful hearts and peaceful consciences, we walk according to the command you gave us, and with illuminated minds, we give you thanks. We hold our lamps in our hands, we take off our old self and, following Your example, we put on the new one; we radiate with Your illuminating teachings, and we cross from darkness to the eternal Light You promised us.

With the prophet David, we cry saying: During the day, we are enlightened by Your teachings, and at night we walk behind You as a Column of Fire; our minds and thoughts are enlightened by You; as we do deeds of justice. You have made us worthy to accept the life-giving Passion of Your only Son Who became for us the Harbor of Salvation. With the Wise Virgins, we meet You with lighted lamps, filled with the oil of good deeds, instead of the fading lamps which we hold now in our hands.

In Your glorious Kingdom, You will light the lamps of our souls with oil of love, purity of heart, serenity of conscience, and complete freedom. We will offer glory to You, to Your only Son, and to Your Holy Spirit, now and forever.

MZMOORO

All things hidden will be revealed. All kinds of secrets will be known. What was said in secret proclaim it in loud voice What was darkness will become light for you. All days and nights of my life, I meditate upon the word of the Lord, hope for all generations.

READING

Hebrews 6:1–9

Brothers and Sisters:

Let us go on toward perfection, leaving behind the basic teaching about Christ, and not laying again the foundation: repentance from dead works and faith toward God, instruction about baptisms, laying on of hands, resurrection of the dead, and eternal judgment. And we will do this, if God permits.

For it is impossible to restore again to repentance those who have once been enlightened, and have tasted the heavenly gift, and have shared in the Holy Spirit, and have tasted the goodness of the word of God and the powers of the age to come, and then have fallen away, since on their own they are crucifying again the Son of God and are holding him up to contempt.

Ground that drinks up the rain falling on it repeatedly, and that produces a crop useful to those for whom it is cultivated, receives a blessing from God. But if it produces thorns and thistles, it is worthless and on the verge of being cursed; its end is to be burned over.

Even though we speak in this way, beloved, we are confident of better things in your case, things that belong to salvation.

Praise be to God always!

HOLY GOSPEL

Matthew 21:17–27 The Cleansing of the Temple

Let us be attentive to the Gospel of Life and Salvation of our Lord Jesus Christ, as recorded by the apostle Matthew.

The Apostle Matthew writes:

Jesus left them, went out of the city to Bethany, and spent the night there. In the morning, when he returned to the city, he was hungry. And seeing a fig tree by the side of the road, he went to it and found nothing at all on it but leaves. Then he said to it, "May no fruit ever come from you again!" And the fig tree withered at once.

When the disciples saw it, they were amazed, saying, "How did the fig tree wither at once?" Jesus answered them, "Truly I tell you, if you have faith and do not doubt, not only will you do what has been done to the fig tree, but even if you say to this mountain, 'Be lifted up and thrown into the sea,' it will be done. Whatever you ask for in prayer with faith, you will receive."

When he entered the temple, the chief priests and the elders of the people came to him as he was teaching, and said, "By what authority are you doing these things, and who gave you this authority?" Jesus said to them, "I will also ask you one question; if you tell me the answer, then I will also tell you by what authority I do these things. Did the baptism of John come from heaven, or was it of human origin?"

And they argued with one another, "If we say, 'From heaven,' he will say to us, 'Why then did you not believe him?' But if we say, 'Of human origin,' we are afraid of the crowd; for all regard John as a prophet." So they answered Jesus, "We do not know."

And he said to them, "Neither will I tell you by what authority I am doing these things."

This is the truth.

✠ Peace be with you.

Tuesday of Holy Week
Coming to the Harbour

SEDRO

O Immortal One, through Your death You gave life to our race. Send down Your love toward our feeble supplication. O Son of God, You willed to give us life and You died for our sake. Hear the petitions which we bring before You. O Abundant Treasury, from which all who are needy may receive, grant our request which we ask of You. Accept the incense, which we offer before Your majesty; and by it, may the richness of Your fragrant mercies rest upon us.

O Lord, look upon us, Your worshippers standing before You, with souls in agony, and bodies in affliction. Nothing can help, and nothing can save, except Your mercy; and none can heal, and none can give life, except Your love.

As we have borne Your seal since the waters of baptism, have believed in Your Name, and have consumed Your Body and drank Your Blood, let Your living Cross be a rudder for our ship, and guide us through the storms which surround us.

Shine Your salvific mercy upon us; and, by Your grace, let there be rest to our affliction. Let Your mercy bring comfort to us as we bow before You, forgive our sins, and blot out our offenses from Your Book.

When the thread of our life comes to an end, send to us, O Lord, an angel of peace in Your Providence. Let the watcher of Your mercy kindly guide our souls away from the guards and the attacks of the devil, that we may be delivered by You.

Sprinkle upon us the dew of Your mercy and aid, and together with the legions of the children of light, we shall sing glory when You rise to carry out judgement upon all the generations.

In Your mercy, O Lord, make us worthy to stand at Your right hand. Together, we shall all sing glory to Your Divinity and give thanks in a clear voice to You, the Hidden One: Father, Son, and Holy Spirit, one God, to You be glory; and may mercy be upon us, forever.

MZMOORO

The Merciful Physician came to bind up those who suffer. He gave health to all who are afflicted, and healing to all who are sick. Almighty God forever, by the wounds and sufferings which You bore, You healed the wounds of our weak human race, and You forgave our sins and follies. Grant us, Lord, forgiveness of sins from Your treasury. Heal our sins and have mercy on us, that we may sing glory to Your Divinity.

READING

1 Thessalonians 2:13–17

Brothers and Sisters:

We constantly give thanks to God for this: that when you received the word of God that you heard from us, you accepted it not as a human word, but as what it truly is, the word of God, which is at work in you who believe. For you, brothers and sisters, became imitators of the churches of God in Christ Jesus that are in Judea, for you suffered the same things from your own compatriots as they did from the Jews, who killed both the Lord Jesus and the prophets, drove us out, displeased God, and opposed everyone by hindering us from speaking to the Gentiles so that they might be saved. In this way they have continually filled up the measure of their sins, and God's wrath has come upon them at last.

As for us, brothers and sisters, though we were separated from you for a short time—in person, not in heart—we longed with great eagerness to see you face to face.

Praise be to God always!

HOLY GOSPEL

Luke 13:22–30 The Narrow Way

Let us be attentive to the Gospel of Life and Salvation of our Lord Jesus Christ as recorded by the evangelist Luke.

The Evangelist Luke writes:

Jesus went through one town and village after another, teaching as he made his way to Jerusalem. Someone asked him, "Lord, will only a few be saved?" He said to them, "Strive to enter through the narrow door; for many, I tell you, will try to enter and will not be able. When once the owner of the house has got up and shut the door, and you begin to stand outside and to knock at the door, saying, 'Lord, open to us,' then in reply he will say to you, 'I do not know where you come from.' Then you will begin to say, 'We ate and drank with you, and you taught in our streets.' But he will say, 'I do not know where you come from; go away from me, all you evildoers!' There will be weeping and gnashing of teeth when you see Abraham and Isaac and Jacob and all the prophets in the kingdom of God, and you yourselves thrown out. Then people will come from east and west, from north and south, and will eat in the kingdom of God. Indeed, some are last who will be first, and some are first who will be last."

This is the truth.

✠ Peace be with you.

Wednesday of Holy Week
Rite of the Lamp

SEDRO

Exalted an awesome Lord you lived among us, became our brother and showed us the way to salvation. You drank the bitter cup of suffering for our redemption. With enlightened consciences and pure hearts we cry out proclaiming: blessed be your holy life-giving passion that has freed us from the slavery of sin and the power of evil.

Blessed be your holy life-giving passion that has shown the way to salvation. Blessed be your holy life-giving passion that has transformed our weakness into strength and our loneliness into glory.

Now O suffering Lord Jesus who overflows with love for us, we employ you, with the fragrance of this incense, to adorn us with your passion rather than with a royal purple robe, and with your nakedness rather than with a crown, and with your cross rather than with a sceptre. Make our souls purer than snow that we may be dressed in clothes appropriate for your heavenly feast, where we will glorify and thank you with a glory and thanks worthy of your majesty and perfection together with the Father and the Holy Spirit forever.

MZMOORO

Our Lord Jesus entered Zion for the great feast. He was ready to endure pain that would save us. Out of envy leaders made plans to kill God's Son, who had entered holy Zion for the great feast. We now suffer with you,

Jesus, in your passion. Make us joyful, O Redeemer, when you rise.

READING

Hebrews 2:5–12

Brothers and Sisters:
God did not subject the coming world, about which we are speaking, to angels. But someone has testified, "What are human beings that you are mindful of them, or mortals, that you care for them? You have made them for a little while lower than the angels; you have crowned them with glory and honor, subjecting all things under their feet."

Now in subjecting all things to them, God left nothing outside their control. As it is, we do not yet see everything in subjection to them, but we do see Jesus, who for a little while was made lower than the angels, now crowned with glory and honor because of the suffering of death, so that by the grace of God he might taste death for everyone.

It was fitting that God, for whom and through whom all things exist, in bringing many children to glory, should make the pioneer of their salvation perfect through sufferings. For the one who sanctifies and those who are sanctified all have one Father. For this reason Jesus is not ashamed to call them brothers and sisters, saying, "I will proclaim your name to my brothers and sisters, in the midst of the congregation I will praise you."

Praise be to God always!

HOLY GOSPEL

John 11:47–54 Session of the Sanhedrin

Let us be attentive to the Gospel of Life and Salvation of our Lord Jesus Christ as recorded by the apostle John.

The Apostle John writes:

So the chief priests and the Pharisees called a meeting of the council and said, "What are we to do? This man is performing many signs. If we let him go on like this, everyone will believe in him, and the Romans will come and destroy both our holy place and our nation."

But one of them, Caiaphas, who was high priest that year, said to them, "You know nothing at all! You do not understand that it is better for you to have one man die for the people than to have the whole nation destroyed." He did not say this on his own, but being high priest that year he prophesied that Jesus was about to die for the nation, and not for the nation only, but to gather into one the dispersed children of God.

So from that day on they planned to put him to death. Jesus therefore no longer walked about openly among the Jews, but went from there to a town called Ephraim in the region near the wilderness; and he remained there with the disciples.

This is the truth.

✠ Peace be with you.

Thursday of Holy Week
Thursday of the Holy Mysteries

SEDRO

O Christ, you are the Word of the Eternal Father, and you became man to save us. You fulfilled the laws of the old covenant to lead us to worship in spirit and in truth. You washed the feet of your apostles to teach us humility and love. You ate the passover lamb with them, so that you yourself might become our Passover and our Lamb.

We glorify and thank you because you offered yourself for us as an eternal Paschal Sacrifice. You gave us the Mystery of the Holy Eucharist as a pledge of the resurrection and new life.

You shared your eternal Priesthood with the apostles and their successors, priests of the new covenant. Through their hands, you offer yourself to the Father as a pure and acceptable sacrifice.

Now, O Lord, as we commemorate your Last Supper, we ask you, with the fragrance of this incense, to give your Church priests who will offer you in sacrifice, celebrate your Mysteries, and make known your teachings, that your name may be blessed, your kingdom come, and your will be done on earth. Grant forgiveness to sinners and peace to the world. Grant us a good life, so that we may pass safely from this world to everlasting life and in your heavenly kingdom sit with you at the table of your eternal Paschal banquet. We raise glory and thanks to you, to your Father, and to your Holy Spirit, for ever.

MZMOORO

See the true bread, the Lord's Body, that he gave us. Take and eat it for forgiveness and for new life. See our Lord's cup, filled with His Blood, shed to save us. Take and drink it for forgiveness and for new life. Hear the Church call to her children with devout faith: "Come, receive the Gift that Christ gave, and give Him praise."

READING

1 Corinthians 11:23-32

Brothers and Sisters:
I received from the Lord what I also handed on to you, that the Lord Jesus on the night when he was betrayed took a loaf of bread, and when he had given thanks, he broke it and said, "This is my body that is for you. Do this in remembrance of me." In the same way he took the cup also, after supper, saying, "This cup is the new covenant in my blood. Do this, as often as you drink it, in remembrance of me." For as often as you eat this bread and drink the cup, you proclaim the Lord's death until he comes. Whoever, therefore, eats the bread or drinks the cup of the Lord in an unworthy manner will be answerable for the body and blood of the Lord.

Examine yourselves, and only then eat of the bread and drink of the cup. For all who eat and drink without discerning the body, eat and drink judgment against themselves. For this reason many of you are weak and ill, and some have died. But if we judged ourselves, we would not be judged. But when we are judged by the Lord, we are disciplined so that we may not be condemned along with the world.

Praise be to God always!

HOLY GOSPEL

Luke 22:1-23 The Last Supper

Let us be attentive to the Gospel of Life and Salvation of our Lord Jesus Christ as recorded by the evangelist Luke.

The Evangelist Luke writes:

The festival of Unleavened Bread, which is called the Passover, was near. The chief priests and the scribes were looking for a way to put Jesus to death, for they were afraid of the people. Then Satan entered into Judas called Iscariot, who was one of the twelve; he went away and conferred with the chief priests and officers of the temple police about how he might betray him to them. They were greatly pleased and agreed to give him money. So he consented and began to look for an opportunity to betray him to them when no crowd was present.

Then came the day of Unleavened Bread, on which the Passover lamb had to be sacrificed. So Jesus sent Peter and John, saying, "Go and prepare the Passover meal for us that we may eat it." They asked him, "Where do you want us to make preparations for it?" "Listen," he said to them, "when you have entered the city, a man carrying a jar of water will meet you; follow him into the house he enters and say to the owner of the house, 'The teacher asks you, "Where is the guest room, where I may eat the Passover with my disciples?"' He will show you a large room upstairs, already furnished. Make preparations for us there."

So they went and found everything as he had told them; and they prepared the Passover meal. When the hour came, he took his place at the table, and the apostles with him. He said to them, "I have eagerly desired to eat this Passover with you before I suffer; for I tell you, I will not eat it until it is fulfilled in the kingdom of God."

Then he took a cup, and after giving thanks he said, "Take this and divide it among yourselves; for I tell you that from now on I will not drink of the fruit of the vine until the kingdom of God comes." Then he took a loaf of bread, and when he had given thanks, he broke it and gave it to them, saying, "This is my body, which is given for you. Do this in remembrance of me."

And he did the same with the cup after supper, saying, "This cup that is poured out for you is the new covenant in my blood. But see, the one who betrays me is with me, and his hand is on the table. For the Son of Man is going as it has been determined, but woe to that one by whom he is betrayed!" Then they began to ask one another, which one of them it could be who would do this.

This is the truth. Peace be with you.

✠ Peace be with you.

Friday of Holy Week
Signing of the Chalice

PROCLAMATION

Behold the holy Chalice, God's life-giving blood which is consecrated for all mortals by the apostles.

Behold the Chalice of salvation, God's living blood. Come forward all peoples and rejoice for it absolves those who partake of it.

Behold the Chalice which satisfies the thirst of the children of God. Those who drink from it are delivered from the flames of Gehenna.

Behold the Chalice which was prefigured by the chosen nation. But when Jesus came in person, other nations welcomed him with joy.

The honorable priest Aaron, prefigured this Chalice when he sprinkled the blood of animals to signify the Blood of the Lord.

The prophet Moses prefigured this Chalice by the lamb's blood which he sprinkled in Egypt to deliver the children of Israel.

Behold the holy Chalice! From the side of the Father's Son the living are born. From his side, open on the cross by a lance, our thirst is satisfied.

Behold, the Church tells the priests to carry it above the altar for the pardon of her children.

Behold the holy Chalice! From it we receive salvation. From it we drink and are made worthy of the pardon of our faults.

Behold, today it is accomplished through the ministry of the true priests, that all nations are saved.

Behold the holy Chalice! King David foretold it, stating: "I will receive the chalice of salvation, and I will call upon the name of the Lord."

Behold, today it is completed on the table of life, that mortals are promised eternal life.

MZMOORO

With great honor Joseph took our Lord's body from the cross. By this action he made known: favor passed from Israel. Hosts of angels stood in awe and in fear beheld the sight. With great honor Joseph took our Lord's body from the cross. Angels sang our Savior's praise as they stood around his tomb. People of the earth proclaimed: "Lord, you saved us by your death!"

READING

Hebrews 12:12-21

Therefore lift your drooping hands and strengthen your weak knees, and make straight paths for your feet, so that what is lame may not be put out of joint, but rather be healed. Pursue peace with everyone, and the holiness without which no one will see the Lord. See to it that no one fails to obtain the grace of God; that no root of bitterness springs up and causes trouble, and through it many become defiled. See to it that no one becomes like Esau, an immoral and godless person, who sold his birthright for a single meal. You know that later, when he wanted to inherit the blessing, he was rejected, for he found no chance to repent, even though he sought the blessing with tears. You have not come to something that can be touched, a blazing fire, and darkness, and gloom, and a tempest, and the sound of a trumpet, and a voice whose words made the hearers beg that not another word be spoken to them. (For they could not endure the order that was given, "If even an animal touches the mountain, it shall be stoned to death." Indeed, so terrifying was the sight that Moses said, "I tremble with fear.")

HOLY GOSPEL

John 19:31-37 The Blood and Water

Let us be attentive to the Gospel of Life and Salvation of our Lord Jesus Christ as recorded by the apostle John.

The Apostle John writes:

Since it was the day of Preparation, the Jews did not want the bodies left on the cross during the sabbath, especially because that sabbath was a day of great solemnity. So they asked Pilate to have the legs of the crucified men broken and the bodies removed. Then the soldiers came and broke the legs of the first and of the other who had been crucified with him. But when they came to Jesus and saw that he was already dead, they did not break his legs. Instead, one of the soldiers pierced his side with a spear, and at once blood and water came out. (He who saw this has testified so that you also may believe. His testimony is true, and he knows that he tells the truth.) These things occurred so that the scripture might be fulfilled, "None of his bones shall be broken." And again another passage of scripture says, "They will look on the one whom they have pierced."

This is the truth.

✠ Peace be with you.

HYMN: On the Cross the Side of Christ

Teshboohto l-Moryo

On the cross the side of Christ was pierced and wounded.

Blood and water flowed from him to pardon all sins. O faithful Church, now draw near to him with open hands to receive these gifts.

Blood and water witness to the truth of Jesus, that he is true God and Man.

This Chalice bless, Lord.

Teshboohto l-Moryo

Moses sprinkled blood and saved the first-born children.

When the angel saw the blood upon the door posts, they were not harmed.

By the blood that flowed from his pure side Jesus saved his Church.

Now upon the altar here his blood is given as a pledge of life to come.

This Chalice bless, Lord.

Friday of Holy Week
Burial of Our Lord

SEDRO

We worship, thank, and praise your divinity, O God, for you created us in your image and formed us in your likeness. We praise your salvation, O Lover of all people. On this Friday you gave us life by your cross and set us free by your death. In the beginning, you completed our creation on a Friday, the sixth day. Your holy hands formed mortal Adam from the dust of the earth, and you molded and created him in your image. From your own mouth you breathed the breath of life into him. Thus he was fashioned in beauty and perfected in knowledge — a marvelous creation!

But in his ignorance, Adam wandered, neglected your command, and was delivered up to judgment. Death now entered to distort the image of your creation. But even after this, O compassionate and loving Lord, your mercy prevailed. On the sixth day, another Friday filled with mysteries, your hands were nailed to the cross; you were humiliated and mocked and your side pierced in order to give new life to the work of your hands, through the blood and water which flowed from your side.

On this Friday of your saving passion and the commemoration of your life--giving cross, the Church petitions you through the mouths of her children with the fragrance of this incense. As in the beginning, you created out of love and then returned to save and give new life, now grant your mercy upon us, the work of your creation. By your cross, grant peace to the whole universe.

By your cross, remove anger and put an end to wars. By your cross, eliminate dissension. By your cross, curb violence and pacify the angry. By your cross, humble the proud, expose the self--serving, and remove the enemy. By your cross, establish your Church in strength and make her monasteries and convents firm. By your cross, purify your priests and exalt the deacons. By your cross, sustain the elderly, subdue the haste of youth, and educate the young. By your cross, pardon sinners, forgive wrongdoers, and guard your flock which now worships you, honors your passion, embraces your wounds and is glorified and exalted by your crucifixion.

Save us and save all your people. Completely perfect us in your strength. Visit us and revive us, so that our image may be renewed and our likeness recovered. May your comfort take away the sadness of our hearts and your compassion dry our tears.

Then we shall wear your glory and be clothed in your light. Make us worthy to meet the day of your resurrection as heirs in the kingdom. Then without ceasing, we shall raise glory to you, now and ever.

MZMOORO

Praise the Mighty One who carries all creation. For he willed to carry his cross and endure pain. Praise the Mighty One who carries earth and heaven. For he willed to carry his cross and endure pain. On this day the Sun of Justice gripped a pillar, while the children of the darkness stood and scourged him.

READINGS

Isaiah 53:7-12

He was oppressed, and he was afflicted, yet he did not open his mouth; like a lamb that is led to the slaughter, and like a sheep that before its shearers is silent, so he did not open his mouth. By a perversion of justice he was taken away. Who could have imagined his future? For he was cut off from the land of the living, stricken for the transgression of my people. They made his grave with the wicked and his tomb with the rich, although he had done no violence, and there was no deceit in his mouth. Yet it was the will of the Lord to crush him with pain. When you make his life an offering for sin, he shall see his offspring, and shall prolong his days; through him the will of the Lord shall prosper. Out of his anguish he shall see light; he shall find satisfaction through his knowledge. The righteous one, my servant, shall make many righteous, and he shall bear their iniquities. Therefore I will allot him a portion with the great, and he shall divide the spoil with the strong; because he poured out himself to death, and was numbered with the transgressors; yet he bore the sin of many, and made intercession for the transgressors.

Hebrews 1:14-16

Brothers and Sisters: Since, then, we have a great high priest who has passed through the heavens, Jesus, the Son of God, let us hold fast to our confession. For we do not have a high priest who is unable to sympathize with our weaknesses, but we have one who in every respect has been tested as we are, yet without sin. Let us therefore approach the throne of grace with boldness, so that we may receive mercy and find grace to help in time of need. Praise be to God always!

HOLY GOSPEL

Luke 22:1-23 The good thief

Let us be attentive to the Gospel of Life and Salvation of our Lord Jesus Christ as recorded by the evangelist Luke.

The Evangelist Luke writes:

When they came to the place that is called The Skull, they crucified Jesus there with the criminals, one on his right and one on his left. Then Jesus said, "Father, forgive them; for they do not know what they are doing." And they cast lots to divide his clothing. And the people stood by, watching; but the leaders scoffed at him, saying, "He saved others; let him save himself if he is the Messiah of God, his chosen one!" The soldiers also mocked him, coming up and offering him sour wine, and saying, "If you are the King of the Jews, save yourself!" There was also an inscription over him, "This is the King of the Jews." One of the criminals who were hanged there kept deriding him and saying, "Are you not the Messiah? Save yourself and us!" But the other rebuked him, saying, "Do you not fear God, since you are under the same sentence of condemnation? And we indeed have been condemned justly, for we are getting what we deserve for our deeds, but this man has done nothing wrong." Then he said, "Jesus, remember me when you come into your kingdom." He replied, "Truly I tell you, today you will be with me in Paradise." It was now about noon, and darkness came over the whole land until three in the afternoon, while the sun's light failed; and the curtain of the temple was torn in two. Then Jesus, crying with a loud voice, said, "Father, into your hands I commend my spirit." Having said this, he breathed his last. When the centurion saw what had taken place, he praised God and said, "Certainly this man was innocent."

John 19:17-30 Jesus gives up his spirit

The Apostle John writes:

Carrying the cross by himself, Jesus went out to what is called The Place of the Skull, which in Hebrew is called Golgotha. There they crucified him, and with him two others, one on either side, with Jesus between them. Pilate also had an inscription written and put on the cross. It read, "Jesus of Nazareth, the King of the Jews." Many of the Jews read this inscription, because the place where Jesus was crucified was near the city; and it was written in Hebrew, in Latin, and in Greek. Then the chief priests of the Jews said to Pilate, "Do not write, 'The King of the Jews,' but, 'This man said, I am King of the Jews.'" Pilate answered, "What I have written I have written." When the soldiers had crucified Jesus, they took his clothes and divided them into four parts, one for each soldier. They also took his tunic; now the tunic was seamless, woven in one piece from the top. So they said to one another, "Let us not tear it, but cast lots for it to see who will get it." This was to fulfill what the scripture says, "They divided my clothes among themselves, and for my clothing they cast lots." And that is what the soldiers did. Meanwhile, standing near the cross of Jesus were his mother, and his mother's sister, Mary the wife of Cleopas, and Mary Magdalene. When Jesus saw his mother and the disciple whom he loved standing beside her, he said to his mother, "Woman, here is your son." Then he said to the disciple, "Here is your mother." And from that hour the disciple took her into his own home. After this, when Jesus knew that all was now finished, he said (in order to fulfill the scripture), "I am thirsty." A jar full of sour wine was standing there. So they put a sponge full of234 the wine on a branch of hyssop and held it to his mouth. When Jesus had received the wine, he said, "It is finished." Then he bowed his head and gave up his spirit.

This is the truth.

✠ Peace be with you.

Saturday of Holy Week
Saturday of the Light

SEDRO

Glory to you, O holy One. You descended from the heavenly dwellings to the earthly depths. In your compassion you took the form of a slave to forgive your servants. You walked on the waves of the sea in order to sanctity Adam, who was created in the image of your majesty.

O Lord, you sanctified those who are impure and with your hyssop you purified sinners and made them whiter than snow. Through your powerful grace, forgive me and your servants, who ask you for the pardon of their faults and the forgiveness of their sins. As you forgave the family of Cornelius through the hand of Simon Peter, the Apostle, in the same way, may pardon of sins descend upon us and upon all the children of your flock, who have been redeemed by your precious blood. We glorify you, your Father, and your Holy Spirit, now and for ever.

MZMOORO

The true love of the father far surpassed his son's great sin. He ran out to embrace him when at last his son came home. Cel: "I have sinned against heaven and before you," said the son. "Though my heart now condemns me, you are greater than my heart." All: When the just offered worship, you were pleased, O Lord our God. Now be pleased with our worship; in your mercy, hear our prayers.

READING

Romans 5:1-11

Brothers and Sisters:
Since we are justified by faith, we have peace with God through our Lord Jesus Christ, through whom we have obtained access to this grace in which we stand; and we boast in our hope of sharing the glory of God. And not only that, but we also boast in our sufferings, knowing that suffering produces endurance, and endurance produces character, and character produces hope, and hope does not disappoint us, because God's love has been poured into our hearts through the Holy Spirit that has been given to us. For while we were still weak, at the right time Christ died for the ungodly. Indeed, rarely will anyone die for a righteous person — though perhaps for a good person someone might actually dare to die. But God proves his love for us in that while we still were sinners Christ died for us. Much more surely then, now that we have been justified by his blood, will we be saved through him from the wrath of God. For if while we were enemies, we were reconciled to God through the death of his Son, much more surely, having been reconciled, will we be saved by his life. But more than that, we even boast in God through our Lord Jesus Christ, through whom we have now received reconciliation.

Jeremiah 31:31-35

The days are surely coming, says the Lord, when I will make a new covenant with the house of Israel and the house of Judah. It will not be like the covenant that I made with their ancestors when I took them by the hand to bring them out of the land of Egypt — a covenant that they broke, though I was their husband, says the Lord. But this is the covenant that I will make with the house of Israel after those days, says the Lord: I will put my law within them, and I will write it on their hearts; and I will be their God, and they shall be my people. No longer shall they teach one another, or say to each other, "Know the Lord," for they shall all know me, from the least of them to the greatest, says the Lord; for I will forgive their iniquity, and remember their sin no more. Thus says the Lord, who gives the sun for light by day and the fixed order of the moon and the stars for light by night, who stirs up the sea so that its waves roar — the Lord of hosts is his name.

Zechariah 1:1-6

In the eighth month, in the second year of Darius, the word of the Lord came to the prophet Zechariah son of Berechiah son of Iddo, saying: The Lord was very angry with your ancestors. Therefore say to them, Thus says the Lord of hosts: Return to me, says the Lord of hosts, and I will return to you, says the Lord of hosts. Do not be like your ancestors, to whom the former prophets proclaimed, "Thus says the Lord of hosts, Return from your evil ways and from your evil deeds." But they did not hear or heed me, says the Lord. Your ancestors, where are they? And the prophets, do they live forever? But my words and my statutes, which I commanded my servants the prophets, did they not overtake your ancestors?

2 Corinthians 5:16-21

Brothers and Sisters:
From now on, therefore, we regard no one from a human point of view; even though we once knew Christ from a human point of view, we know him no longer in that way. So if anyone is in Christ, there is a new creation: everything old has passed away; see, everything has become new! All this is from God, who

reconciled us to himself through Christ, and has given us the ministry of reconciliation; that is, in Christ God was reconciling the world to himself, not counting their trespasses against them, and entrusting the message of reconciliation to us. So we are ambassadors for Christ, since God is making his appeal through us; we entreat you on behalf of Christ, be reconciled to God. For our sake he made him to be sin who knew no sin, so that in him we might become the righteousness of God.

Praise be to God always!

HOLY GOSPEL

Matthew 27:62-66 The Guard at the Tomb

Let us be attentive to the Gospel of Life and Salvation of our Lord Jesus Christ as recorded by the apostle Matthew.

The Apostle Matthew writes:

The next day, that is, after the day of Preparation, the chief priests and the Pharisees gathered before Pilate and said, "Sir, we remember what that impostor said while he was still alive, 'After three days I will rise again.' Therefore command the tomb to be made secure until the third day; otherwise his disciples may go and steal him away, and tell the people, 'He has been raised from the dead,' and the last deception would be worse than the first." Pilate said to them, "You have a guard of soldiers; go, make it as secure as you can." So they went with the guard and made the tomb secure by sealing the stone.

Matthew 18:15-22 Forgive one another

Let us be attentive to the Gospel of Life and Salvation of our Lord Jesus Christ as recorded by the apostle Matthew.

The Lord Jesus says:

"If another member of the church sins against you, go and point out the fault when the two of you are alone. If the member listens to you, you have regained that one. But if you are not listened to, take one or two others along with you, so that every word may be confirmed by the evidence of two or three witnesses. If the member refuses to listen to them, tell it to the church; and if the offender refuses to listen even to the church, let such a one be to you as a Gentile and a tax collector. Truly I tell you, whatever you bind on earth will be bound in heaven, and whatever you loose on earth will be loosed in heaven. Again, truly I tell you, if two of you agree on earth about anything you ask, it will be done for you by my Father in heaven. For where two or three are gathered in my name, I am there among them." Then Peter came and said to him, "Lord, if another member of the church sins against me, how often should I forgive? As many as seven times?" Jesus said to him, "Not seven times, but, I tell you, seventy-seven times."

This is the truth.

✠ Peace be with you.

Resurrection Sunday

Scripture Readings, Prayers, & Meditation from the Fathers

Resurrection Sunday
Christ is Risen! Alleluia!

SEDRO

We worship and praise you, O Only Begotten Son. You descended into the darkness of the tombs and worked wonders in the realms of the dead. By your resurrection you freed the captives, and by your voice you awakened the righteous and the just who had gone to their rest in the sleep of death. You gathered the nations to worship you and to proclaim your salvation. They rejoice and cry out.

On Friday the king endured pain and was crucified, and today victory has been achieved by his resurrection. On Friday a lance pierced his side, and today in his compassion the waters of baptism flow. On Friday he was crowned with thorns, and today he has adorned his church with a crown of splendor.

Today is the day of rejoicing in the resurrection. Today is the day of rejoicing for all who have gone to their rest in the hope of the resurrection. Today, with the fragrance of this incense, the church and her children celebrate and sing hymns of glory, saying, O Creator of life, you have saved us by your passion and have given us life by your resurrection.

Now renew our image by your grace. Clothe our bodies with the power of the Spirit, so that we may shine in the robe of glory and in its light see you, the true Bridegroom. In your grace make us and all the faithful departed worthy of your heavenly kingdom, that we may raise glory and thanks to you, to your Father, and to your Holy Spirit, forever.

MZMOORO

Peace and hope have been given to all people far and near, from the tomb Christ has risen, gathering his flock as one. Now the church is rejoicing, for her shepherd truly rose. Christ, who died for his people, conquered death to give new life. Lord our God, you accepted what the just had offered you. Now accept in your mercy our pure sacrifice and prayers.

READING

1 Corinthians 15:12-26 Christ the First fruits

Brothers and Sisters:
If Christ is proclaimed as raised from the dead, how can some of you say there is no resurrection of the dead? If there is no resurrection of the dead, then Christ has not been raised; and if Christ has not been raised, then our proclamation has been in vain and your faith has been in vain. We are even found to be misrepresenting God, because we testified of God that he raised Christ — whom he did not raise if it is true that the dead are not raised. For if the dead are not raised, then Christ has not been raised. If Christ has not been raised, your faith is futile and you are still in your sins. Then those also who have died in Christ have perished. If for this life only we have hoped in Christ, we are of all people most to be pitied. But in fact Christ has been raised from the dead, the first fruits of those who have died. For since death came through a human being, the resurrection of the dead has also come through a human being; for as all die in Adam, so all will be made alive in Christ. But each in his own order: Christ the first fruits, then at his coming those who belong to Christ. Then comes the end, when he hands over the kingdom to God the Father, after he has

destroyed every ruler and every authority and power. For he must reign until he has put all his enemies under his feet. The last enemy to be destroyed is death.

Praise be to God always!

HOLY GOSPEL

Mark 16:1-8 The Resurrection of Jesus

Let us be attentive to the Gospel of Life and Salvation of our Lord Jesus Christ as recorded by the evangelist Mark.

The Evangelist Mark writes:

When the sabbath was over, Mary Magdalene, and Mary the mother of James, and Salome bought spices, so that they might go and anoint him. And very early on the first day of the week, when the sun had risen, they went to the tomb. They had been saying to one another, "Who will roll away the stone for us from the entrance to the tomb?" When they looked up, they saw that the stone, which was very large, had already been rolled back. As they entered the tomb, they saw a young man, dressed in a white robe, sitting on the right side; and they were alarmed. But he said to them, "Do not be alarmed; you are looking for Jesus of Nazareth, who was crucified. He has been raised; he is not here. Look, there is the place they laid him. But go, tell his disciples and Peter that he is going ahead of you to Galilee; there you will see him, just as he told you." So they went out and fled from the tomb, for terror and amazement had seized them; and they said nothing to anyone, for they were afraid.

This is the truth.

✠ Peace be with you.

MEDITATION FROM THE SYRIAC FATHERS

Let us, therefore, strive by faith and excel in every virtue to gain after this life that clothing so that when we lay aside our body we will not be naked and that there will be nothing in that day to glorify our flesh. For insofar as anyone, through faith and zeal, has been deemed worthy to receive the Holy Spirit, to that degree his body also will be glorified in that day. What the soul now stores up within shall then be revealed as a treasure and displayed externally in the body. It is something like the trees once winter has passed. They are warmed by the invisible power of the sun and winds. The trees shoot outwardly and send out leaves and flowers and fruit like external clothing. Similarly also in spring flowers of the plants blossom forth from within the bosom of the earth and the earth is thus covered and decorated. The plants are like those lilies described by the Lord that "not even Solomon in all his glory was arrayed as one of these" (Mt 6:29). For all examples of this nature are types and images of Christians at the resurrection.

So to all God-loving souls, I mean, true Christians, there is the first month, which is called April. This is, indeed, the day of resurrection in which, by the power of the Sun of Righteousness, the glory of the Holy Spirit rises up from within, covering and warming the bodies of the saints. This is the glory they interiorly had before, hidden in their souls. For what they now have, that same then pours out externally into the body. This, I say, is the first month of the year (Ex 12:2). This brings joy to every creature. It clothes the naked trees; it opens the earth. This produces joy in all animals. It brings mirth to all. Now for Christians April, the first month, the time of the resurrection in which their bodies will be glorified by means of the light which even now is in them hidden, this is the power of the Spirit who will then be their clothing, food, drink, exultation, gladness, peace, adornment, and eternal life. For the Divine Spirit, whom they were considered worthy even now to possess, will then bring about in them every beauty of radiance and heavenly splendor.

Macarian Homilies, Homily 5

Safro & Ramsho

Morning and Evening Prayer for Daily Personal Use Selected from the Maronite Divine Office

✟ Safro ✟
(Morning Prayer)

PRE-OFFICE PRAYERS

In the name of the Father, Son and Holy Spirit, the one true God. Amen.

We profess, adore, and glorify the holy and glorious Trinity: Father, Son, and Holy Spirit. Amen.

Qadishat Aloho,
Qadishat Hyeltono,
Qadishat Lomooyoto,
ItraHam aleyn!

Our Lord, have mercy upon us.
Our Lord, have compassionate mercy on us.
Our Lord, receive our worship and our prayers, and have mercy on us.

Our Father, who art in heaven, hallowed be thy name. Thy kingdom come. Thy will be done, on earth as it is in heaven. Give us the bread of our daily need. Forgive us our debts and sins as we forgive our debtors. Lead us not into temptation, but deliver us from evil. For thine is the kingdom and the power and the glory unto the ages of ages. Amen.

Hail Mary, full of grace, Our Lord is with you. Blessed are you amongst women and blessed is the fruit of your womb, Our Lord, Jesus Christ. Holy Mary, mother of God, pray for us now and at the hour of our death. Amen.

PSALM 51

Have mercy upon me, O God, according to Your loving-kindness; according to the multitude of Your tender mercies blot out my transgressions.

Wash me thoroughly from my iniquity, and cleanse me from my sins;
for I acknowledge my transgressions, and my sin is ever before me.

I have sinned against You, against You alone.
I have done what is evil in Your sight. Your judgments are right. Your sentence is just. For behold, I was born in iniquity; and in sin when my mother conceived me.

But You take delight in the truth. You have made known to me the secrets of your wisdom. Sprinkle me with Your hyssop, and I shall be clean; wash me and I shall be whiter than snow.

Fill me with Your joy and gladness, that my bones, which are crushed, may rejoice. Turn Your face away from my sins, and blot out all my iniquities.

Create in me a pure heart, O God, and renew a right spirit within me. Cast me not away from Your presence; and take not Your Holy Spirit from me.

Restore to me the joy of Your salvation; and uphold me with Your glorious Spirit; then I will teach transgressors Your way, and sinners shall turn to You.

Deliver me from blood-guilt, O God, the God of my salvation, and my tongue shall praise Your righteousness. O Lord, open my lips, and my mouth shall sing Your praises.

For You desire not sacrifices, You are not appeased by burnt offerings. The sacrifices of God are a humble spirit; a broken and a contrite heart, O God, / You will not despise.

By Your loving-kindness do good to Zion; build up the walls of Jerusalem. Then You shall be pleased with the sacrifices of righteousness, with burnt offerings and whole burnt offerings; then they shall offer bullocks upon Your altar.

To you belongs praise, O God. Barekhmor.

SOOGHITO

Oh my beloved, children of the Church, give glory at this time of morning. Every morning we profess and worship the Good One who has ordered all the luminaries in the heavens.

The veil lifted from the regions of the world and His light has dawned upon creation. The dawn of morning awakens those asleep; may Your shining light illumine our hearts.

Let us, our Lord, speak Your glory, and be for us the treasure of life within our souls. As You bring us out from the darkness, so likewise deliver us from Gehenna.

In Your compassion, freely feed the children of the Church who cling to You. May Your compassion be an advocate for us, Lord of the dawn and of all times.

May Your goodness accompany us and may we arrive at Your great dawn. May Your right hand pour mercy upon us and by it may we cross over the sea of fire.

O Just One who requites all justly, do not make my account by justice. Be for me, rather, a Companion of mercy, my Savior, and with You I will arrive at the harbor of life.

When I am judged by fire sprinkle me with Your dew like as to the Holy Youths in the furnace of Babylon. The fire roars upon the wicked – include me with Your holy ones, O Lord.

Medicine that remedies all ills, heal our wounds with the medicine of Your mercy. To the company of Abraham, Isaac and Jacob the righteous ones include me, O Lord.

May Your body and blood be a guide to me and by them may I be delivered from conflagration. May Your cross be a bridge to all of us and may we cross over the chasm of terror.

We rise now. Lo! We call to You, may we hear Your voice, "Come ye blessed of my Father." The Exalted One who is full of compassion and mercy, exalt us, Lord, on the day of Your coming.

Heaven and earth, and all in them profess with us our restoration. Thanksgiving be to You, the worshipful Father, and to Your Only-Begotten Son and to the Holy Spirit.

Let us all say every morning: glory be to You for your many mercies: and let us say at every moment your prayers are with us, O Mother of our Lord.

To the Father and to the Son and to the Holy Spirit may we raise glory at every moment: for His unspeakable gift, unto the age of ages. Amen and amen.

Stomen kalos! Kyrie eleison!

PETITION OF MOR JACOB

Open to us Your door full of mercy, Son of God; hear our petitions and have mercy upon our souls. Peace of peace to heavenly and earthly beings, grant peace to

Your Church and preserve her children by the cross of light.

Dawn upon me, our Lord, and I will be illumined by You like the day. I will luminously sing Your glory as I marvel. May morning awaken me to the glory of Your divinity and deeper intimacy with You the whole day through.

With the daybreak, may Your light dawn upon my thoughts and may it drive out the shadows of error from our souls. Creation will be illumined; with it, illumine our hearts and they will glorify You both day and night.

Lo! The dawn bears pure incense, which we offer to You. We offer it to You with all due thanksgiving for by Your command the slumber of night has passed away from us. Pass away with it the sin that beats and wounds us.

The mornings and evenings glorify You, Our Lord, in their alternation. The priests and deacons of all the Church offer to You sweet incense; they glorify You. Glory be to Him who enlightens us with His stately light.

May the Virgin Mary, who bore You, intercede on our behalf to You. Through the prayers of the beloved company of prophets, apostles and martyrs have compassion on the weak, heal the sick, forgive the dead and to us sinners remit our debts. Our Lord who magnifies the remembrance of Your Mother and holy ones, through their prayers forgive us, Lord, and our departed. Through the prayers of Your Mother with the prophets, apostles and martyrs protect the living and forgive the departed in Your mercy.

HOOTOMO

Kyrie eleison! Kyrie eleison! Kyrie eleison!

Glory be to You. Glory be to You. Glory be to You.

O God, who are our heavenly Father, by Your living and holy name guard us from evil and bring us not into trial, You who are our hope in every hour. We call to You, our Lord and God; to You be glory forever.

>Amen.

May our feeble service, O Lord our God, be to Your satisfaction, our prayers find favour in Your sight, our supplications to Your majesty, mercy, compassion, assistance, goodness and love perfected in Your divinity so that they may come, dwell, and be poured upon our weakness and sinfulness in both worlds created in Your goodness. Our Lord and God, to You be glory forever.

>Amen.

✟ Ramsho ✟
(Evening Prayer)

PRE-OFFICE PRAYERS

In the name of the Father, Son and Holy Spirit, the one true God. Amen.

We profess, adore, and glorify the holy and glorious Trinity: Father, Son, and Holy Spirit. Amen.

Qadishat Aloho,
Qadishat Hyeltono,
Qadishat Lomooyoto,
ItraHam aleyn!

Our Lord, have mercy upon us.
Our Lord, have compassionate mercy on us.
Our Lord, receive our worship and our prayers, and
have mercy on us.

Our Father, who art in heaven, hallowed be thy name. Thy kingdom come. Thy will be done, on earth as it is in heaven. Give us the bread of our daily need. Forgive us our debts and sins as we forgive our debtors. Lead us not into temptation, but deliver us from evil. For thine is the kingdom and the power and the glory unto the ages of ages. Amen.

Hail Mary, full of grace, Our Lord is with you. Blessed are you amongst women and blessed is the fruit of your womb, Our Lord, Jesus Christ. Holy Mary, mother of God, pray for us now and at the hour of our death. Amen.

PSALM 51

Have mercy upon me, O God, according to Your loving-kindness; according to the multitude of Your tender mercies blot out my transgressions.

Wash me thoroughly from my iniquity, and cleanse me from my sins;
for I acknowledge my transgressions, and my sin is ever before me.

I have sinned against You, against You alone.
I have done what is evil in Your sight. Your judgments are right. Your sentence is just. For behold, I was born in iniquity; and in sin when my mother conceived me.

But You take delight in the truth. You have made known to me the secrets of your wisdom. Sprinkle me with Your hyssop, and I shall be clean; wash me and I shall be whiter than snow.

Fill me with Your joy and gladness, that my bones, which are crushed, may rejoice. Turn Your face away from my sins, and blot out all my iniquities.

Create in me a pure heart, O God, and renew a right spirit within me. Cast me not away from Your presence; and take not Your Holy Spirit from me.

Restore to me the joy of Your salvation; and uphold me with Your glorious Spirit; then I will teach transgressors Your way, and sinners shall turn to You.

Deliver me from blood-guilt, O God, the God of my salvation, and my tongue shall praise Your righteousness. O Lord, open my lips, and my mouth shall sing Your praises.

For You desire not sacrifices, You are not appeased by burnt offerings. The sacrifices of God are a humble spirit; a broken and a contrite heart, O God, / You will not despise.

By Your loving-kindness do good to Zion; build up the walls of Jerusalem. Then You shall be pleased with the sacrifices of righteousness, with burnt offerings and whole burnt offerings; then they shall offer bullocks upon Your altar.

To you belongs praise, O God. Barekhmor.

SOOGHITO

Light your lamps, my brothers, so as to meet the Bridegroom who is coming.

In the Garden of Eden shall the souls of the just dwell on the day of recompense.

The feast of light shall be open to them and they shall glorify Him with their harps.

All who have awaited Him and hoped in His name will dance joyously to meet Him when He comes again.

Lo! Meet the Bridegroom who is coming. Blessed the one who is awaiting Him.

A crown of glory is woven for the just who await His name and His salvation.

The First-Born was moved and descended to Sheol to raise the dead from their graves.

The righteous beheld His light in Sheol and longed to meet the compassionate Son.

Their sicknesses and suffered passions were forgotten as they beheld their Lord hung upon the wood.

He gave us life due to His mercy, and so our mortality is raised to stand amidst the watchers.

Death lied in ambush for our humanity. In His goodness, Our Lord came and saved us.

Glory be to You, Lord of watchers, who gladdened the downcast of Sheol by Your dawning Light.

Therefore night fled and was ceased! And His Light dawned upon creation.

He descended from the high place, saved us and ascended. Lo! He, again, sits on the right hand of the Father.

All who have awaited Him and hoped in His name long to meet Him when He comes again.

His light dawned upon Sheol and drove away the darkness from the departed therein.

The fruit that Adam consumed killed him, but the fruit that descended from on high saved him.

The graves burst open and the dead arose. Let this for us a pattern of the great day.

Draw near and meet Him on the day of resurrection. Blessed the one who is awaiting Him.

Great is the day on which He will come. On it, all hidden things will be revealed.

Those who have lain down in the dust will hear His voice on the day of resurrection and go out to meet Him.

Adam marveled when he was resurrected and returned to the place full of blessed things.

Let us all say every evening glory to You for Your many mercies: and let us say at every moment your prayers are with us, O Mother of our Lord.

To the Father and to the Son and to the Holy Spirit may we raise glory at every moment: for His unspeakable gift, unto the age of ages. Amen and amen.

Stomen Kalos! Kyrie Eleison!

PETITION OF MOR JACOB

Lord, our Lord, Lord of watchers and of angels, hear our petition and have mercy on our souls. Peace of peace to heavenly and earthly beings, grant peace to Your Church and preserve her children by the cross of light.

In the time of evening, where is the light of daytime? For darkness spreads and evening shadows are upon the four quarters of the earth. In the habitation of Sheol, where is the great world? For here one dwells in obscurity and where there is nothing which will be nothing.

Lo! Evening is sent to every man, he sleeps and he sees all that he owns is left behind. The garment of everyone will be taken away from him and he will be naked as death leaves all stripped of their possessions.

Morning dawns and it brings fresh garments to clothe them – prefigured in it is the resurrection of the dead in great amazement. Know now who strips the twilight gloom off of you. Lo! He brings the dawn to you to clothe Your limbs.

Awaken us, Lord, from entanglements in this world and prepare us to inherit life with Your holy ones. Grant us to be clothed in garments fitting to the house of the righteous ones. Prepare us pleasing cloaks of virtue.

Glory be to You, Lord, who separated night from day and made them to represent proverbs and parables.

Thanksgiving be to You, Lord of times and seasons, all of which are fleeting to You who is without end.

We remember the prophets, the apostles and the martyrs. We remember those who have diligently cultivated the vineyard of our Lord. We remember St. Jacob, St. Maron, his companions, and St. Ephrem, the Harp of the Holy Spirit. Through their prayers have pity on the weak, visit the sick, forgive the dead, and to us sinners, remit our debts.

We magnify, our Lord, the remembrance of Your Mother and all Your holy ones. Through their prayers forgive us, Lord, and our departed. Through the prayers of Your Mother with those of the prophets, apostles and martyrs preserve the living and forgive the departed in Your mercy.

HOOTOMO

Kyrie eleison! Kyrie eleison! Kyrie eleison!

Glory be to You. Glory be to You. Glory be to You.

O God, who are our heavenly Father, by Your living and holy name guard us from evil and bring us not into trial, You who are our hope in every hour. We call to You, our Lord and God; to You be glory forever.

    Amen.

May our feeble service, Lord our God, be to Your satisfaction, our prayers find favour in Your sight, our supplications to Your majesty, mercy, compassion, assistance, goodness and love perfected in Your divinity so that they may come, dwell, and be poured upon our weakness and sinfulness in both worlds created in Your goodness. Our Lord and God, to You be glory forever.

    Amen.

www.ingramcontent.com/pod-product-compliance
Lightning Source LLC
Chambersburg PA
CBHW070621050426
42450CB00011B/3098